Redefining Normal:
A Real World Guide to Raising an Autistic Child

(Written for Autism Parents by an Autism Parent)

Also from Brooke Price

'Living Through Autism's Eyes: My Journey with My Son, 2nd Edition'

'8 Simple Steps to IEP Success'

'Beautiful Disasters: A Look Inside of Bipolar Disorder'

Redefining Normal:

A Real World *Guide to Raising an Autistic Child*

Brooke Price

Another World Publishing **Washington** ©2014

For the parents that just discovered they are part of the ASD family. Keep persevering, one day your sense of hopelessness will become your sense of solace.

Disclaimer:

AWP and their author, Mrs. Brooke Price, officially state that Mrs. Price is not a medical doctor. All information in this book has been obtained from research, experience as an autism mother, and interviews. Thank you.

Contents

Acknowledgments

When I get an idea in my head, a book I want to write, I start writing and tend to lose track of the world. I forget any responsibilities I have. Except my children of course. This particular book came out of a spontaneous idea. I sat down and started in. In this time, per usual, I have lost track of everything. I think I owe a few people a thank you for being so understanding. Many thanks and much gratitude to my two Co- administrators for our Autism Support Group- Thank you guys so much for picking up my slack. To my friends that I mostly ignored. You guys rock, thanks for your unwavering support. I'd also like to thank my sons, each member of my support group, all the people that have become personal friends through our connection to autism, all members of AWP, Judi for keeping me on track. My mom, my dad, Tawana, my siblings-all one zillion of you, ha-ha, my grandparents, my aunts and uncles. My parents. Mostly I want to thank Chaz, for, well, everything one person can thank another for.

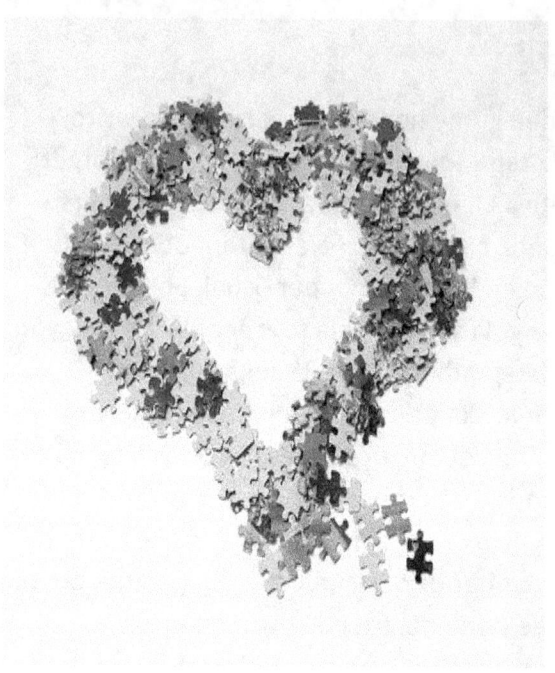

Picture Courtesy of Google Images

"You suddenly realize the value of friendships. People that you thought would always stick around and be there for you suddenly stop calling, and eventually drop off the face of the earth. However you establish new connections with other parents and people that understand. I have learned to value these new friendships and have come to realize that they are worth more than anything else in this world."

Author Unknown

Chapter 1

Questioning Everything

There can't be a precise way to describe the feelings that sweep over you as you are told your child/children have autism. You feel utter hopelessness, confusion is often felt as well. More than anything it seems, in the beginning, parents seem to feel **_denial_**. It seems easier to argue against it in their head while looking for reasons the doctor was wrong than it is to accept it. Then they tend to feel the most dominant feeling, they became **_angry_**.

In my case I was angry at my husband for not understanding my stress, with the doctor for not being more thorough in explaining what autism was to mad, at the school system for never mentioning it to me even though it seemed quite obvious that they knew; most of all I felt angry with myself. I mean, come on, I'm supposed to know my son better than anyone and I couldn't figure this out. I was angry because this had to be my fault. Angry because it was like they were telling me that I did something wrong. Angry that it felt like all my hopes and dreams for my child were ruined, ripped away from me during an hour long appointment.

There are a number of spectrum parents that felt the exact same way when their child/children were diagnosed. It's natural for this to happen to a parent. It is like they're telling you that your whole family is going to change.

A few weeks after finding out you'll moved on to aggressively trying **_to figure out how this happened, how I could've stopped it._** Wondering if there's anything you have done. If I had gotten him to a doctor a little sooner would he have been less severe. Maybe if I had paid more attention to his milestones.

Through meeting and speaking to other parents that are traveling a road much like other spectrum parents you learn that this step is almost universal. Most parents you will meet strongly bargained with their own god to make their child better or thought about the things they believe they did wrong. As parents we put blame on ourselves, as mothers we put ten times as much naturally.

You will also hear a lot of parents talking about falling into a **_deep depression_** not long after their child's diagnosis. Most worry about whether their child will regress and obsessed over not being a good enough parent to raise their child. They pity themselves for having been thrust into this new life. They worry about how they're going to pay for the medical expenses. As time passes you'll start worrying about money. After all it is estimated to take around $2.3 million, in the U.S., on average for lifetime care of an autistic.

Finally you will **_accept_** it and start trying to find the positive in this new challenge. To deal with this you can spend your time learning about autism and the autism spectrum of disorders. (Autism, Asperger syndrome, pervasive developmental disorder not otherwise specified (PDD-NOS), childhood disintegrative disorder, and Rhett syndrome) Learn about teaching them through PECS's cards and ABA therapy.

Having mixed feelings when your child is diagnosed with any disorder is normal. The thing is figuring out how to navigate through the tunnel of harmony all while making sure you come out the other end victorious and ready to take on the world. Because that is exactly what you are about to do, whether you realize it or not.

Something you may find interesting or ironic; the stages you go through [what I just explained] are the same stages of grief people go through after experiencing a death.

The 5 Stages of Loss and Grief:

Denial/Isolation

Anger

Bargaining

Depression

Acceptance

Finding out that what I was feeling was normal for somebody that had just lost a loved one puts everything into perspective. You are mourning the life you thought you were going to have. Nothing in life is definite and finding out you are about to take a different path is much like losing someone you love. You just lost the identity you have spent years creating, you have to reinvent yourself as a special needs parent. You have to learn how to live by a routine without spontaneity. You have to redefine normal. Realizing this made it easier to accept.

You aren't doing anything wrong. Feel what you feel until you are ready to accept your child's/children's diagnosis. It takes time and the amount of time isn't decided. Every one's path is different. Some take years and some weeks. Whatever speed you move at is on you. Do remember that early intervention is everything to these kids. 25%-50% of kids who receive early intervention, or EI, move on to general education by kindergarten.

Chapter 2

Criticism and Abandonment

Realizing how few people understand your life is one of the hardest realizations for a newly diagnosed special needs family to come to terms with. Your whole world has changed with one doctor's appointment. You have to figure out how to redefine your life and you're routine. When you explain that to society they don't see it as being as big of a deal as it is. Your child's entire ability to function depends on you being able to do everything the same way and keep everything the same in your home. As simple as that sounds, somehow they still do not 'get it'.

It's very hard for most people to grasp how your kids mind works, let alone how it feels to walk alone in our shoes, yet they still offer criticism at every turn. We all know that, the normal public, aren't going to completely understand; it still doesn't make their lack of knowledge acceptable. Autism affects 1 in 50 school aged kids now. Anymore it doesn't pay to be ignorant to this disorder.

Unfortunately people can be cruel, even when they don't mean to be. A lot of the time strangers don't realize that a disapproving look, thoughtless judgment, or impatient nature toward a parent of an individual with autism can be more emotionally upsetting than any somatic pain felt. It doesn't hit you until later that sometimes family and friends have become bigger strangers to you than the man you passed leaving the gas station or the lady that works in the office at the local supermarket. Someone that knows your every move can become just another person you used to know.

If you haven't already noticed it, you will soon. One by one you start to lose friends and family after your child is diagnosed. Not many families haven't had this happen, but no two families are alike. If you don't lose a single social contact then many will be extreme jealousy of you. They would however congratulate you for having exactly what you need to start coping with this disorder as a parent.

The thought of a special needs child turns many people away on its own. Normally ignorant beliefs are what drives them to disappear. It hurts when the person you have sat with for years, hung out with, shared your deepest secrets with or maybe even someone you have known since elementary school all of a sudden stops coming around as much, then not at all. Be prepared for this to happen, even if you believe it never will. That's normal. No one thinks this will happen to them.

You have to keep reminding yourself that you can't help people who don't want to understand. It doesn't happen. You have to learn to become comfortable with the fact that any one that left you behind wasn't there for you to begin with. Also that even though they went on without you you'll have the pleasure of sailing past them with a smile as your child progresses more and more whether it be emotionally, physically, socially, or just behaviorally.

As hard as losing a friend is, it is even harder to slowly realize that some of your family will never get it. They somehow don't even realize how insulting their words are as they are saying them to you. Maybe you've had a family member not allow their child around your's as to decrease the chance that your child's autism will rub off on their kid. Some people report how family members don't believe that their child is autistic because they say that the child isn't better because the mother didn't try hard enough. I mean what is that even supposed to mean?

A number of autistic parents also report ignorance as a problem. Here's an amassed list of the most common phrases said to autism parents. It'll also give you some examples what to say if need be. Most parents say they always wish they'd known what to expect and have tips on how to handle it.

Top 8 Most Insensitive Comments Made to an Autism Parent:

"What's wrong with her/him?"

"Nothing is wrong with him/her. She/he has autism. What's wrong with you?"

"Why do you let him/her do that? She/he is scaring my child"

"I let him/her do that because he/she needs to do it. Maybe you should educate your child about autism, and yourself"

"You know, there is no cure"

"Yes I am aware there is no cure for my child. Did you know there is no cure for bad social skills or ignorance either?"

"Have you tried___? If you did, he/she would be more normal"

"You really think so? Guess I should be paying you for advice instead of the specialists"

"My child doesn't know how to play with your autistic child"

"You mean your child doesn't know how to play with another child? Playing is universal, your child just has to learn to use an imagination with my child"

"Give me your child for a week and I'll whip him/her into shape"

"I am free around 4 today. I'll drop him/her at your front door. Don't be surprised if I burn my tires leaving"

"Your child just needs discipline"

"Ha, if that were true all the boot camps in the world would be ran by the parents of autistics"

"If that were my kid, he'd/she'd be different"

"If he/she was your kid YOU'D be different"

Even if you end up feeling alone and abandoned by the lack of understanding coming from the people around you, there are still people out there you can go to. The force of us parents is growing by the day. We support each other and look out for each other with dedication you've never seen. There is nothing like talking to a likeminded person, someone that walks almost the same path as you.

If you are lucky enough to never have to experience any of this, to have completely understanding and supportive people in your circle then you are luckier than you'll ever know. With that said, other parents would implore you to reach out to other parents like you. It makes all the difference and you learn so much.

This was never going to be simple.

Picture Courtesy of Google Images

Chapter 3

Touching on the Medical Basics

Before your child is diagnosed with autism you most likely never considered what you should do first or how confusing all of it was going to be. Everything is all jumbled in their brain after they are diagnosed. It makes it hard to focus. Every pre-school I called asked me all kinds of questions, none of which I had the answer for. They were speaking another language as far as I was concerned. Plus I looked really bad not knowing a thing. One of the behavioral therapist suggested to me that I keep a behavior folder and keep track of his meltdowns and such. He said that it is the easiest way to identify his triggers and his habits. It was an amazing suggestion, within 3 months I knew his every move and began to predict what he was about to do.

During one of your earlier appointment's your doctor will most likely suggest that you spend some time looking up the terms and what their relevance to autism is. Of course you couldn't have a clue how long of a task that is going to be, but you won't really care. You will began to take on the long task of learning autism. Here is some help to shorten your anxiety toward finding where to search for the simple information that you need.

Autism Term Glossary

-AAC"*Assistive Augmentative Communication*"

A speech-language therapists' term for communication with a picture board or recorded messages buttons

-ABA "Applied Behavior Analysis"

Acronym in common use by adherents of some behavioral techniques to refer to a kind of careful analysis and tracking of behavior

-ABC "Applied Behavior Consultants"

-ABC "Autism Behavior Checklist"

Diagnostic device for autism.

-ADI "Autism Diagnostic Interview"

A diagnostic scale for autism being developed by the Medical Research Council in London

-ADOS "Autism Diagnostic Observation Scale"

(Or "Autism Diagnostic Observation Schedule"?) Fairly technical test.

-AIT

"Auditory Integration Training"

-Apraxia

A neurologically-based disorder which occurs in adults, often as a consequence of stroke. Apraxia may be specific to speech (e.g., "apraxia of speech") or to the movement of other body parts (e.g., "limb apraxia").

-ASD

"Autistic Spectrum Disorders"

-Autistic Spectrum Disorders

Term that encompasses the following five disorders listed in DSM-IV: Autistic Disorder, Asperger's Disorder, PDD-NOS, Childhood Disintegrative Disorder, and Rhett's Disorder.

-CARS "Childhood Autism Rating Scale"

A test developed at TEACCH to diagnose autism. The child is rated in 15 areas on a scale totaling up to 60, ranges are considered to non-autistic, autistic, and severely autistic

-DD

"Developmental Disabilities"

-Echolalia

Repeating back something said to you. Delayed Echolalia is repeating it later. Both behaviors are found in many autistics. Functional echolalia is using a quoted phrase in a way that has shared meaning, like a child who sings the Barney jingle to ask for a Barney videotape, or says "Get your shoes and socks" to ask to go outside.

-IEP

"Individualized Educational Plan"

-LD

"Learning Disabled"

-NIMH

"National Institutes for Mental Health"

-PANDAS

"Pediatric Autoimmune Disorders Associated with Strep"

-PECS

"Picture Exchange Communication System"

-PDD-NOS or PDD/NOS

"Pervasive Development Disorder--Not Otherwise Specified"

-PECS

"Picture Exchange Communication System"

-SLP or S-LP

"Speech-Language Pathologist"

-SI

"Sensory Integration"

-Stim

(E.g. stimming) short for "self-stimulation", a term for behaviors whose sole purpose is to stimulate their own senses.

(wikipedia.com)

In no way conceivable are those 23 terms all the help you need when you first start out or anytime through this journey you're beginning. It does not matter how many pages of information you gather, it will **NEVER** be everything you need. Knowing some of the basic websites with useful information helps as well. The more information you soak up in the beginning the better prepared you will be when you walk in to your first IEP meeting or have to argue with a doctor for the first time. Regrettably you'll find yourself in one of these situations at some time.

A good percentage of parents of autistic children do have the doctor problem too. It becomes very frustrating and very exhausting. Mostly when you get to a point where you realize you know way more about autism than your child's doctor does. In order to help you learn what you need to know, here is a list of websites that can be of help to any spectrum family.

Autism Websites

www.autism-society.org

www.autismspeaks.org

nationalautismassociation.org

www.nimh.nih.gov

www.cdc.gov/ncbddd/autism/links.html

lanproject.org

lancommunity.org

www.cdc.gov/ncbddd/autism/links.html

You should make sure and keep all the paper work from your child's school and doctors. Including a list of medications your child uses or used. It always comes in handy as a reference or a way to make your point. You may find keeping these things to be exceptionally helpful on appointment days when you are frazzled and tend to forget things you meant to say and information you should tell the doctor. Also to be able to answer the doctor's question about past therapy's/medications. If you have all the information right there, often summarized on a piece of paper your appointments will almost always be easier to get through. (Healthline.com)

There are many comorbid diseases to look for as well.

Children with Autism Tend to Have:

Sensory processing disorder

Adhd

Anxiety disorders

Bipolar disorder

Gastrointestinal disorders

Developmental coordination disorder

Fragile X syndrome

Intellectual disabilities

Neuroinflammation and immune disorders

Nonverbal learning disorders

Ocd

Tourette syndrome

Seizures

Tuberous sclerosis.

(Webmd.com)

A ton of autism parents also complain about their children never sleeping. Worst part is giving them some Tylenol Pm or Benadryl doesn't work one bit. There is a large chance that your child will be diagnosed with one or more of these comorbidities sometime after their initial autism diagnosis. It is a hard thing to deal with, but it is common in a lot of disorders other than autism.

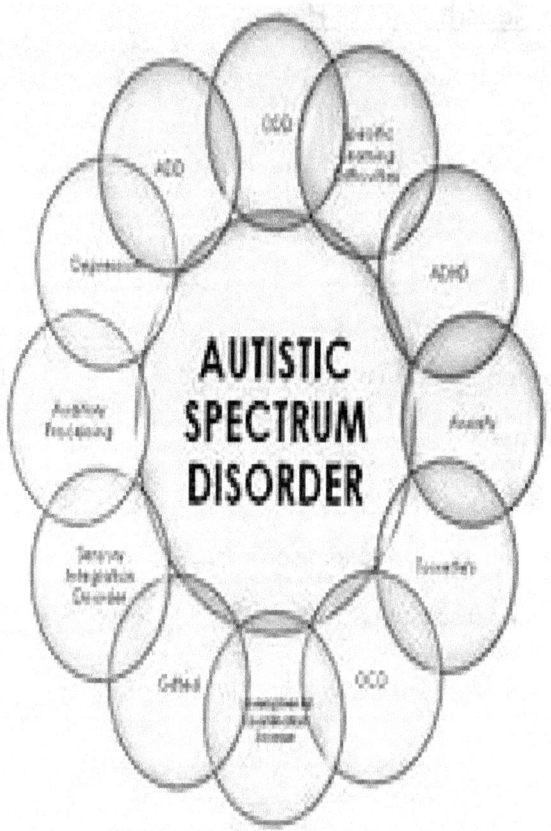

Picture Courtesy of Google Images

Most doctors and specialists recommend doing genetic testing on autistic children to get an idea of whether that child's autism has a genetic link. The technique is called chromosome microarray analysis. According to these doctor's this should be the first step in any attempt to find the cause of a developmental disorder. (Genetics.thetech.org)

Spontaneous alterations in the genetic material during meiosis that delete or duplicate genetic material. They are called CNV or copy number variations and are more common in people who have autism or other neurodevelopmental disorders for example. (wikipedia.com) This is the case with my son. He has a complete duplication of his 8q chromosome.

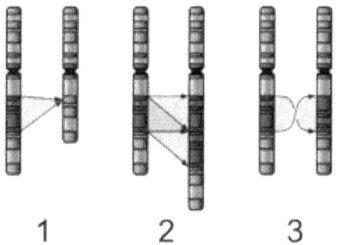

(1)Deletion (2)Duplication (3)Inversion Picture Courtesy of Google Images

Genetic testing is always a scary thought. Not one mother or father out there, when faced with sitting down and hearing the results of their child's genetic testing, are calm and together. It's nerve racking. Secretly you are wondering if the doctor is going to tell you it was your fault, or your spouses, or worse. What if it isn't genetically linked? That puts you back at square one. If this test doesn't explain it you are back to wondering what caused it. It's like you're almost trying to exonerate yourself from any blame all while trying to scream out that it is all your fault and burst into tears just to make it all stop for a minute. Doesn't make much sense, but what does any more anyway?

The question has been asked a lot about finding out if it is one parents fault or not. The only way to find out is to have the parents DNA tested. More often it is CNVs. A large number of autistic individuals with unaffected parents/family members often result from copy number variations. Meaning, the genetic abnormality doesn't have to come from either parent. They have found that a large number of genetic cases are spontaneous duplications or deletions. (Genetics.thetech.org)

I'm not a doctor by any means. I'm an autism mom. I've been for 11 years. It's my life. I live and breathe autism, as you will find it will become the case for you too. It becomes 2nd nature. All the information I've provided in this chapter is purely from experience, research, interviews with other spectrum parents, and from information doctors have given me over the years. If you have any questions or concerns you should **_ALWAYS_** consult your child's doctor.

The doctors you're going to see are going to be mostly psychologists/psychiatrists. There are also developmental pediatricians and neurologists that treat autistic children as well. Most family doctors are not comfortable treating autistic children. I'd warn against using a Family Practice doctor to treat. Finding the proper doctors for my child was a big challenge from the time he was born. In some areas it is not a problem. I have not found any of these places but I am assured they exist.

Normally all faith is lost in the new doctor as soon as you shake their hand. I have even had a specialist tell me that I knew more about autism than they did. Talk about floored. I have also sat in my floor more than once with lists of doctors, trying to find one that would take our insurance. I do hope that this changes for these kids and their parents soon. There is just not enough doctors to go around, not enough doctors that know what they are talking about, and NO doctors that are affordable even with insurance. Honestly, in my opinion, there are not enough doctors left that care.

Logic would suggest that children whose parents can afford private insurance would have better access to mental health and behavioral services and would be less likely to use ERs for such care. The reverse seems to be true. A Kennedy Krieger Institute study thinks that this could be because some private insurance plans do not cover mental health services for autism, strictly limit the number of treatment sessions, or require patients to see a small number of network providers. (Iancommunity.com)

If a child has a bad meltdown or bout of self-injury, a parent may have no other place to go for urgent care than the ER. This visit may cost more than $1,200 for them where it would be free for someone with state insurance. (Iancommunity.com)

Parts of the Brain
Affected by Autism

Cerebral Cortex:
A thin layer of gray matter on the surface of the cerebral hemispheres.
Two thirds of this area is deep in the tissues and folds. This area of the
brain is responsible for higher mental functions, general movement,
perception and behavioral reactions.

Amygdala:
This is responsible for all
emotional responses including
aggressive behavior.

Basal Ganglia:
This is gray masses deep within
the cerebral hemisphere that
connectes the cerebrum and the
cerebellum. It helps regulate
automatic movement.

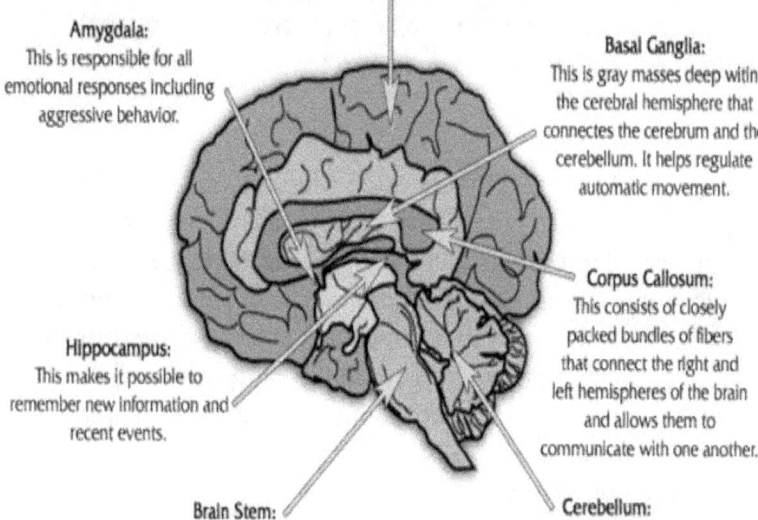

Corpus Callosum:
This consists of closely
packed bundles of fibers
that connect the right and
left hemispheres of the brain
and allows them to
communicate with one another.

Hippocampus:
This makes it possible to
remember new information and
recent events.

Brain Stem:
The Brain Stem is located in front of the cerebellum
and serves as a relay station, passing messages
between various parts of the body and the cerebral cortex.
It controls the primitive funtions of the
body essential to survival including breathing and heartt rate.

Cerebellum:
This is located at the back of the brain, It
fine tunes motor activity, regulates balance,
body movements, coordination and
the muscles used for speaking.

Picture Courtesy of Google Images

Chapter 4

Challenging Behaviors

The challenging behaviors associated with autism are often exceptionally hard for a parent to cope with; it's emotionally draining. For a new autism parent the norm is to be overwhelmed and to be searching for answers. For someone to say, "Yeah, I've been there, you aren't alone." You know, someone to connect with, someone to give them guidance.

The veteran autism parent tends to be a little calmer about the challenges. They have had time to soak in some info and learn to set routines and implement calming techniques. The pros have been at this for a decade or more. They are forces to reckon with. These parents can predict meltdowns and overloads like its second nature. Yet sometimes some of these challenges still overtake them. My point is, no matter how long you've been at this, whether you are a beginner or a pro you are going to have hard days.

Autism has several core challenges that are associated with it. They are broken down into 3 categories.

Social/Communication Problems

Social Issues: little to no eye contact, not seeking out social situations or people, focusing more on objects than people, lacking theory of mind or understanding that other people need attention outside of your own agenda. (NIMH.com)

Communication Issues: unable to make small talk nor understand why it is necessary, not being able to pick up social queues, in some cases not even having speech or having impairments of it. (NIMH.com)

Repetitive Behaviors/Restricted Interests

Obsessions: Individuals with autism tend to have very narrow interests. Depending on their age it can be dinosaurs to stamps, etc. They often carry on and on about these obsessions and do not talk much about anything else. (NIMH.com)

Stimming: Repetitive and sometimes Self-Injurious Behaviors: Stimming is something that most autistic individuals do to calm themselves. It is normally flapping of the hands or spinning, sometimes playing with the fingers. As long as these behaviors do not become self-injurious there is no problem in them stimming. However if the stimming does become harmful you need to call a doctor. Examples of what is meant by self-injurious: hand biting, head banging, or scratching. (NIMH.com)

Insistence on Sameness: Often autistics are very dependent on sameness, on having a routine. They like to be able to predict what is going to happen next. It is like a sense of control and a sense of comfort. Some even have rituals like having to line up the same toys in the same order or having to have pictures straight and where they stay, or having to have the same towel each time they bathe, some even requiring driving the same way every time you go to the store. This is very important to them.

Other Challenging Issues

Comorbid disorders: As mentioned in chapter 3

Sleep Problems and other Sleep Issues: Sleep issues are almost universal with autism. The severity of the issues are different in each child. Some kids have trouble falling asleep, some staying asleep. Some stay up all night, literally. Some only get up once. Melatonin helps a large number of them, some need stronger medications, some the doctors can't find medicines to help. (NIMH.com) It is very draining to parents and child.

Sensory Issues: This describes the issues that some autistics have processing the world around them. They have increased response to their 5 senses, so much so that in some cases they use 2 extra senses. They are called the *proprioceptive sense* (knowing what your muscles and joints are doing and where you are in space) and the *vestibular sense* (related to the inner-ear and involves your awareness of movement, head position, and balance). (researchautism.net) Also the sensory issues explain why autistic children set blankly when someone is talking and have no response to the fact they are being spoken too. Like they are deaf.

Mood Instability and Meltdowns: In a toddler and in an older child, it gets labeled a "meltdown"; in an older teen or adult high functioning enough to be out on their own it may result in getting fired or being arrested. In some cases, they become aggressive to others and/or destroys property during their fit, it is a major problem. (autism.about.com) This is usually caused by the inability to communicate, broken routines, items out of order, sensory overload, and the unfathomable behavior of other human beings. Autistic meltdowns often result in either the child or the parent being hurt.

Motor Skills Issues: This refers to gross motor skills like large muscles and actions like lifting your head, sitting up, or riding a bike. Fine motor skills involve small, precise motor movements, like holding a crayon or picking up a penny. These impairments are much worse than they sound. It is much harder to interact with peers if you can't ride a bike, catch a ball, or run well. It has an effect on what you can do with kids in the neighborhood, at recess, or in gym. (NIMH.com)

Executive Function Issues: This is referring to an autistic individual's ability to organize and be flexible. Both children and adults with an ASD often find it difficult to cope with the demands of work or school in terms of being prepared. Like knowing what is due when, and keeping track of where needed materials or assignments are. Just getting ready in the morning can be a challenge. Autistics often find help is very much needed in this area. (NIMH.com)

Activities of Daily Living: Many people on the spectrum find it hard to learn organization and flexibility. (wikipedia.com)

Some of these core issues can be helped with medications, some with vitamins, some with repetition, PECS cards/ABA, and some are just things you are going to have to come to terms with. These things will be the things you'll learn to love.

Chapter 5

Medications vs. No Medications

A number of parents decide that going the holistic route is the proper path for them. They normally choose a doctor called a DAN! Doctor. Defeat Autism Now (DAN!) is a project of the Autism Research Institute. It was founded in the 1960s by Dr. B. Rimland. DAN! Doctors are trained in the "DAN! Protocol," This is an approach to autism treatment that starts with the belief that autism is a biomedical disorder. DAN! Doctors feel that autism is a disorder caused by a combination of lowered immune response, external toxins from vaccines, and problems caused by certain foods. (wikipedia.com)

Some of the Major Interventions Suggested by DAN! Practitioners:

Nutritional supplements: like certain vitamins, minerals, amino acids, and essential fatty acids

Special diets totally free of gluten (from wheat, barley, rye, and possibly oats) and free of dairy (milk, ice cream, yogurt, etc.)

Testing for hidden food allergies

Treatment of intestinal bacterial/yeast overgrowth (with pro-biotics)

Detoxification of heavy metals through chelation (a hazardous medical procedure)

(wikipedia.com)

Just so you have full disclosure, DAN! Doctors are credentialed medical doctors who choose to attend a one-day DAN! Training. There is no further credentials, testing, or follow up. According to a spokesperson for the Autism Research Institute:

"We make every attempt to provide a comprehensive seminar for practitioners teaching them techniques for assessing, testing and treating children on the spectrum using the biomedical approach. We are now insisting anyone on the ARI Clinician's Registry attend at least one training or conference every two years. However, due to the overwhelming legal ramifications, we do not "certify" any practitioner." (autism.com)

Despite knowing how these doctors are trained you have to acknowledge that there are thousands of parents who claim that their children were cured of autism because of the DAN! Protocol. We will never know if their claims are true- there is no doubting some children have done well under the care of DAN! Physicians and clinicians. (autism.com)

DAN! Doctors have one thing right millions of autism parents use the gluten free diet for their kids. The diet is super confusing at first and extremely restrictive as to what can and cannot be eaten.

A gluten free diet consists of excluding the protein gluten from the food you eat. Gluten is found in grains like wheat, barley, rye and triticale (a cross between wheat and rye). It is as expensive a diet as it is restrictive. Some of the things you should stay away from unless they are marked 'gluten free' are:

Beer, Breads, Cakes and Pies, Candies, Cereals, Cookies and crackers, Croutons, French fries, Gravies, Imitation meat or Seafood, Matzo, Pasta, Processed luncheon meats, Salad dressings, Sauces, including soy sauce, Seasoned rice mixes, Seasoned snack foods, such as potato and tortilla chips, Self-basting poultry, Soups and soup bases, and Vegetables in sauce. A whole lot of no-no's aren't listed. That doesn't even cover it all. (NIMH.com)

This diet may be beneficial to your child, so if the time comes that you face the decision of whether or not to try a gluten free diet; remember that no matter how big a pain it is or how silly it sounds to remove a certain protein to help your child that it also may be exactly what you are looking for. While using this diet parents reported improvements in their children's/child's behavior, better digestive health, and improved eye contact, etc.

Another treatment method that parents often use is medicating their children. No one knows for sure how many children with autism are medicated, but the estimates are around 50%. (Iancommunity.com) Medications are often key components in the treatment of a child on the spectrum. Compared to other treatments, medications have the most evidence supporting their use.

The most used medications in the treatment of ASD's and the purpose of their uses are as follows:

Antipsychotic Drugs: These are more commonly used to treat psychotic symptoms from schizophrenia, bipolar disorder, depression and other mental health disorders. Psychotic symptoms include hallucinations and delusions. In ASDs, some of the newer antipsychotics ("atypical antipsychotics") are used for irritability and behavioral problems, such as aggression, self-injury, and rapid mood swings.

Atypical antipsychotics used in autism:

-Risperidone (Risperdal)

-Clozapine (Clozaril)

-Olanzapine (Zyprexa)

-Quetiapine (Seroquel)

-Ziprasidone (Geodon)

Other antipsychotics commonly used in autism include:

-Aloperidol (Haldol)

-Chlorpromazine (Thorazine)

-Apriprazole (Abilify) (Webmd.com)

Antidepressants: These are used to treat depressive disorders but many are also effective treatment for anxiety disorders and Obsessive Compulsive Disorder. They are also used for ADHD, bedwetting and smoking cessation. Most antidepressants work by changing the levels of specific chemicals in the brain called neurotransmitters. Some of the things being targeted by these drugs include aggression, self-injurious behavior, anxiety, agitation, over activity, and some stereotypical behaviors.

SSRIs used in autism:

-Fluvoxamine (Luvox, Faverin)

-Fluoxetine (Prozac, Fontex, Seromex, Seronil, Sarafem)

-Sertraline (Zoloft, Lustral, Serlain)

-Paroxetine (Paxil, Seroxat, Aropax, Deroxat, Paroxat)

-Citalopram (Celexa, Cipramil, Emocal, Sepram, Seropram),

-Escitalopram (Lexapro, Cipralex, Esertia)

TCAs used in autism:

-Clomipramine (Anafranil)

-Desipramine (Norpramine)

Amitriptyline (Elavil, Endep)

-Imipramine (Tofranil)

Other antidepressants used in autism: venlafaxine (Effexor) (Webmd.com)

Stimulants: These are used to treat Attention Deficit Hyperactivity Disorder (ADHD). They use these drugs because many children with autism show the same symptoms as kids with ADHD. These drugs are available in short-acting and long-acting formulas. How central nervous system (CNS) stimulants work isn't completely understood, the medication is thought to target the brainstem arousal system and the cortex.

Psychostimulants used in children with autism: -- Amphetamine mixed salts (Adderall, Adderall XR), -Methylphenidate XR (Concerta, Metadate CD), dextroamphetamine (Dexedrine)

-Methylphenidate (Ritalin)

(Webmd.com)

Mood Stabilizers: This group is used to treat bipolar disorder in both children and adults. Other uses include behavioral symptoms such as aggression, self-injury, impulsivity and conduct disorder. Many anti-seizure medications have mood-stabilizing properties too. Only a few of these types of drugs have been studied in children with autism. Definitive, reproducible results are not available.

Mood stabilizers possibly used in autism:

-Lithium

-Lamotrigine (Lamictal)

-Valproic Acid (Depakene, Depakote)

-Carbamazepine (Tegretol)

-Topiramate (Topamax)

-Oxcarbazepine (Trileptal)

-Levetiracetam (Keppra)

(Webmd.com)

Anticonvulsants: This group treats seizures which occur in as many as one-third of children with autism. Despite the lack of specific evidence supporting their use, anticonvulsants are prescribed for children with ASD

Anticonvulsants used in children with autism:

-Phenytoin (Dilantin)

-Clonazepam (Klonopin)

-Carbamazepine (Tegretal)

-Valproic Acid (Depakote, Depakene)

There are other medications targeting the central nervous system being used for children with autism. The following is a partial list of other medications being used in autism.

Other medications used in autism:

-Alprazolam (Xanax, Niravam), buspirone (Buspar)

-Lorazepam (Ativan)

-Naltrexone (Vivitrol)

-Diazepam (Valium)

-Melatonin

-Antihistamines(Webmd.com)

Figuring out the proper route to take is tricky for every family. Once autism families find what works for them they tend to advocate for it fiercely. Trying to get as many people as possible to know that their way is very important to them. We all have to experiment, use trial and error. We have to feel the days out to eventually figure out what to do. In the end though, no matter what you decide, getting treatment for your child is 100% necessary.

Chapter 6

The Infamous Cause and Cure Debates

The cause debate and the cure debate are the two most hotly debated points in autism life. Of course this opinion could be debated itself, most people would agree though. The debates are pretty well self-explanatory. Parents of autistic children, scientists, and autistic adults are split as to the causes of autism and if a cure is necessary. Almost everybody eventually joins a side in both of these debates and they hold their belief close to their heart. Debates over both topics have been seen to turn very hostile very fast.

Starting with the cause debate. There are three basic groups that you should know about in this topic. The first group is what I call 'The scientific group'. These individuals tend to be at great odds with the next group that will be explained. The scientific group believes that there is NO autism epidemic. They do not believe that vaccines are an issue and in some cases they do not buy the genetics explanation. They always argue the points of testing criteria being added and the diagnosis criteria being altered. From 1980-1993 there were 6 diagnosing criteria for autism. In 1994 scientists added 16 optional points. This added a lot of room for error in their opinions. This group seems to be more accepting of the environmental beliefs a long with the paperwork change adding to the diagnosis numbers. So basically, the numbers aren't really going up according to them, we are just misdiagnosing.

The second group is what I call 'The McCarthy group'. These people take the stance that most autistic children are autistic because of vaccines. To be more specific, the mercury in the vaccines. To be even more specific, the thimerosal. Thimerosal is 49% ethyl mercury. The vaccine that this group set their focus on in the beginning was the MMR vaccine (measles, mumps, and rubella). For around 5 years this was their primary focus. (Vactruth.com) In 1999 they removed the mercury containing thimerosal. It was left in some flu vaccines and in a lot of vaccines used overseas still though. (wikipedia.com)

These individuals tend to dismiss any federal rulings or CDC announcements out of nonbelief. A lot of people from this group even go as far as saying that the government has some conspiracy against the families of autistics.

The third group are individuals do not buy into the 'McCarthy' beliefs, they also do not put very much weight into the 'Scientific' beliefs either. They do, however, put a little more stock into the 'Scientific' belief. The most prominent people that belong to this group are the founders of the AutismSpeaks foundation. These people look at autism as a disease, not a disorder. (autismspeaks.org) As you would expect most scientist do not support their beliefs. They act as if autism is a virus that needs to be treated; not like autism is a disorder you have to live with, manage, and love.

The Cause debate is always a touchy one. No one really knows for sure. If they did we'd have a lot more options as far as treatment. There are so many different thoughts. There is no surprise that there's so much confusion. For example, here are:

Some of the Different Possible Causes:

-Genetics

-Age of the parents

-Nutrition

-Prenatal environment

-Ethanol

-Thyroid problems in the mother

-Inadequate iodine

-Smoking

-Herbicides

-Taking folic acid

-High testosterone levels in the amniotic fluid

-Ultrasounds

-Low birth weight

-Bleeding on the infants brain

-Lack of vitamin D

-Vaccines

-Tylenol after the MMR vaccine

-Mother withholding affection or a 'refrigerator mom'

-The herpes virus

-Multiple sclerosis

(researchautism.net)

No matter which one speaks the truth, the matter at hand is that the prevalence is growing. The numbers are actually astonishing.

The other debate most often talked about in the autism community is the cure debate. This debate is extremely touchy with all involved. You have to consider the High Functioning autistics and the more challenged autistics as well as the parents. The main issue that can be seen is that each one of those people look at autism in a different light.

The higher functioning autistic are normally on the side opposing a cure. It is like if they had a cure it would be like trying to get rid of them. If you cure the autism then you cure the part that makes them who they are. They would rather have more understanding for what they go through and more acceptance of them as people. In fact one website quoted a high functioning young man as saying, "We don't need to be cured, and we just need tolerance and understanding!" (blogs.redorbit.com)

The more impaired autistic individual tends to be more in favor of a cure. They want nothing more than to be able to function at a higher level. Not all of them follow this line of thinking, but a large number do. The same website quoted a moderately functioning autistic man as saying, "Enough with the awareness, we need a cure and fast!" (blogs.redorbit.com)

Deciding if there is something 'wrong' with an autistic individual seems to be a large point of interest in this conversation. They debate whether autistics should be helped or if they should be cured. If they are dangerous or if they are fine.

You also have the parental side of it. Some parents are strongly on the cure side of it. Some are strongly on the anti-cure side of it. Most autism parents say that they just want their kid to be happy, no matter what that takes or what it happens to be. That's all they care about. Makes you stop and think for a moment. This is a desperate battle that cannot be won in any sense. For one, there's no cure, so what point is there in fighting over whether there should be a cure or not.

Second, why are we fighting over something that is obviously none of our business? If there were a cure it would most certainly be each autistic individual's choice whether or not to take it. The whole debate over both seems redundant to me. The cause debate is more relevant to our plight now. We need to pinpoint what causes this in order to be able to help it. That is only my opinion as a parent.

If you form an opinion on either side of these debates I implore you to make sure you look up both sides in depth. Get a good sense for each side of each debate. Once you decide, have dedicated yourself to it, and always be open to swaying one way or another. No treatment or belief is set in stone when it comes to autism.

Chapter 7

A Whole New Look at School

That old picture of school in your head. The one that remembers it as being boring or exciting, a place to escape or a burden. It is easy to remember all the basketball games and football too. The dances and recesses, getting a break from our parents. That is not the memories you are going to have of your child's school after your first few IEP meetings (IEP stands for Individualized Education Plan). School for an autistic child and their parent can be a very challenging time. The amount of time you have to put into your child's education almost quadruples once your child is diagnosed. Before school starts you are going to want to contact the district's special education department and inform them of your child's autism and any comorbid disorders. They will inform you as to what to do to have your child qualified for special needs services.

First thing you are going to want to do after you have everything squared away with the special education department is to show your child their room and route to their classroom a few times before school actually begins. This should be rather easy to set up with your child's principal. You are going to want to also meet your child's teachers and therapists as well as getting email addresses and phone numbers. Also write the names of each person you talk to down for future reference.

Before the first day of school write down all concerns you are having. Pin that paper up somewhere and through the first month of school before your very first IEP meeting. (autismspeaks.org) Legally every school has up to 30 days to hold the first IEP meeting of the year. In that 30 days or until the appointment day, write down any concerns that you are seeing surrounding transportation, recess, in any class, homework, testing, therapies, transitions, etc. Always have a list of things that you want to bring up at the IEP and remember to try to stay as held together as possible.

Some of these meetings can end up being very emotional. Some case conference committees are tremendously professional and very interested in helping your child progress. Some, however, are in it for funding and to do the least amount of work they can do. You HAVE to watch out for that. No matter what kind of school system it is, having an IEP for your child is a must.

As it gets close to your IEP meeting you will get a paper sent home with you child. It gives you a time and date for your meeting. You will have to sign the paper and notate that you will be attending by checking a box. You will hold this meeting with your child's general education teacher, your child's special education teacher, your child's therapists (OT, SLP, etc.), a representative of the district (such as the principal), somebody to interpret the meaning of the IEP papers to the parent (if needed), and any advocate brought by the parent (if necessary). You will have to work together as a team, or try to, in order to give your child the best education you can.

Most parents have no clue what an IEP meeting is the first time they hear of it, let alone what you do during one. It is confusing, 'normal' children's parents never have to do this. The short explanation of what an IEP is would be that it's a document put together by the parents and teachers of a special needs child. The document is meant to protect the child's best interests in making sure they have the services they need. It also binds the school system to provide the services listed in the IEP or face legal recourse.

During IEP meetings you discuss many different areas. You will go over **your child's present levels**. This means they show you how your child is currently doing in school and how their disability affects their progress in the general curriculum. They will also go over the goals for your child, basically what the teachers think your child is capable of in that year.

Next will come the **related services to be provided to your child**. This is talking about if your child requires a 1 on 1 aide, or Para. Also if they need a communication device. That would be covered in this section. They will discuss **how much of each day your child will spend in special education vs. General education.** Now a days schools push for inclusive classrooms, meaning putting special needs children in regular classrooms for part of the day.

You'll have to talk about whether your child is **to take the district-wide assessments**, if so, what modifications your child needs to be able to make it a successful test for your child.

Your child's school will also have to discuss **when any modifications and therapies will start** and explain **how the school officials will push for your child** to meet their goals.

In addition to the issues just discussed they will bring up whether your child's behavior interferes with their learning or others learning. The IEP team will talk about strategies and/or support to address the child's behavior. If your child has limited proficiency in English. They will talk about the child's language needs and how these needs relate to their IEP. If your child is blind or visually impaired: They must provide instruction in Braille or the use of Braille, unless it determines after an appropriate evaluation that your child doesn't need this. If your child has communication needs. They must consider the needs. If your child is deaf or hard of hearing. They will consider the child's language/communication needs. If your child needs assistive technology devices or services.

The school will have you sign several spots if you agree to everything in the IEP in front of you. In some cases you will only see a draft. The official document will be typed up and sent to you to sign and send back. Now it's time for to start implementing the special requirements and class schedules that were discussed during the meeting. Unfortunately the law does not give a specific amount of time the IEP team needs to get everything implemented by. The law specifically states that they only have to implement all the points "as soon as possible after the IEP is developed". (autismspeaks.org)

Other huge problems that some parents and children find are rooms called quiet rooms, schools not allowing GPS devices on the student if it includes a recording device and abuse from teachers and aids. Exclusion rooms are padded rooms with locked doors that the teachers use to calm an autistic child during a meltdown. There have been cases where children have been left in these tiny rooms all day, forgotten about. They find them hungry, scared, and soiled.

This is not a common occurrence by any means. However happening once is enough to be concerned and outraged. One of the very first questions I ask whenever I talk to the special education teacher or the principal for the first time is if their school uses exclusion rooms.

The GPS issue has been debated. It's unclear why some schools do not allow these devices. For children that wander this device is lifesaving. Some also record the day and send the recordings to the parent's emails. The schools that have admitted that they do not allow these devices if they have the recording devices. They say that it is a breach of confidentiality for the other students and the teachers. Some autism parents believe this is a way for the school to cover itself in the case that abuse is recorded.

The last big problem is the abuse of special needs students. There has been cases of students being held down, hit, called names, left in quiet rooms, and restrained. Unless you secretly send a recording device or video recording device it is extremely hard to prove this is happening, especially in the cases of nonverbal students.

In 2004 there was an incident of a special needs boy named Johnathan. His teacher gave him a belt to hold up his pants then later locked him in the quiet. Johnathan hung himself with the belt. We have to stop these things from happening. (myfoxal.com) The problem is that no one has an acceptable answer. There are even reports that teachers have been locking kids in the room over simple things like tapping their desks or crying. Seclusion rooms or quiet rooms have slowly been phased out, but some schools still use them.

Examples of Quiet Rooms; Pictures Courtesy of Google Images

Normally schools are helpful and supportive of autism families but you should by all means watch out for signs of this happening, Such as behavioral changes. Also keep record of everything. If you don't feel like you can handle a situation on your own you can always call an advocate. They will give you advice or even possibly come with you to address the issue and help you protect your child's best interests. The last steps you can take are to make emergency services, family members, and your child's school aware of your child's behaviors and their wandering patterns if you have figured them out yet. You could also enroll you child in swimming lessons in order to lower the chances of wandering and drowning.

Chapter 8

The Number One Cause of Death of our Children

"When it comes to our children there are few things more devastating than your child not meeting their milestones followed by finding out your child has an incurable disorder" was the response when one scientist was asked about the fears of an autism parent. (Healthline.com) One of those more devastating fears to think about or experience for parents is wandering. It is a large fear of mine as well.

Autistic children are prone to wandering from their home or from their parent in public. There are also cases of autistic children wandering off from school. One of the more notable cases is the disappearance of a child named Avonte in New York. He wandered from school and wasn't found for 3-4 months. When they found him he was dismembered and dumped near the Green River in Queens.

In April 2013 a 3 year old little girl was found near a body of water in Massachusetts. The next day she was pronounced dead.

A month later a larger search was launched over three days as hundreds of emergency service personnel and volunteers searched around Clearlake, Calif., looking for 9-year-old Mikaela Lynch, she had wandered from her backyard. The outcome grimly echoed the Wareham search. A dive team found Mikaela's body in a muddy creek.

The body of 11-year-old Anthony Kuznia, was found in April in the Red River after a 24-hour search near his home in East Grand Forks, Minn.

These 3 cases are 3 of the 14 cases of autistic children wandering and being found dead just this year alone.

(nbcnews.com)

The CDC says the prevalence is at 1 in 68, and a federal survey this year says that the prevalence is at 1 and 50 schoolchildren —that is more than 1 million children collectively. As you talk about the prevalence raising you should look back through the years. Even back to the 70's you can see the definite rise in the disorder.

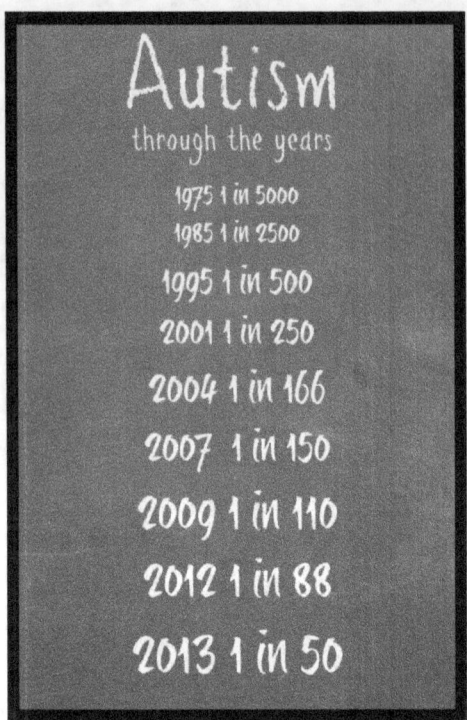

Picture Courtesy of Google Images

Wandering caused the deaths of over 60 children in four years; the fear it induces in the hearts of all parents of autistic child is enough to consume your whole day. This is one of the largest reason for the parental issue of the GPS devices not being allowed in classes.

"We take steps at home — locks on every door, gates, alarms," said writer Jo Ashline of Orange, Calif. Jo's 11-year-old son has autism. "But there's always, in the forefront of our minds, the thought that one tiny mistake could prove fatal."

(autism.about.com)

Advocate groups want to raise awareness. Some of these groups are The National Autism Association and Autism Speaks. They are now making their priority to raise awareness of wandering to the parents and professionals who deal with autistic children, and the first-responders that handle missing-children cases. According to one autism website a study in Pediatrics found out that half of parents with an autistic child had never received advice or guidance on how to deal with possible wandering.

One of those parents trying to change that is Sheila of Colwich of Kansas. Sheila's 5-year old son, Mason, drowned in a pond in July 2010 after squirming out of the family home through a window that had been raised around half a foot because their air conditioner had went out. (ezinearticles.com)

You need to always be aware that this could possibly be a problem in the future and prepare your home and your family for what to do in the event of your child wandering. Keep an ID card for your child and a recent picture at all times. Wandering is one of the very first things you should address when your child is diagnosed. This is not always a problem for families but for the ones that do have to be concerned it is one of their biggest fears as a special needs family.

Chapter 9

The Affect Autism has on Siblings

The biggest reason for the issues surrounding siblings of autistic children is rooted in the need their sibling have for the parent's attention. It tends to leave the neurotypical sibling feeling left out or not as loved or resentful. This leads to behavioral issues and depression in some cases. The 'normal' sibling needs the assurance that even though their brother or sister gets most of the attention, that they are going to get some too.

There are several different steps you should always take to insure that your neurotypical child always feels included and just as important to you.

1. Make sure to tell them that you love them every single day

2. Make sure to gives a lot of hugs

3. Try to ensure the work that they bring home from school is not destroyed by their sibling

AND

4. Encourage them to express their feelings

(Yourfamilyclinic.com)

Dealing with this sibling rivalry of sorts can cause parental stress. Raising an autistic is hard enough let alone the doctors, schools, meltdowns, sibling rivalry all combined equals a large amount of stress and tears. Eventually you will be able to handle this stress better, it is normal for autism parents to breakdown every once in a while. It is normal to feel so much stress you just need someone to vent too. This is Ok. It's normal. Over time you get used to it, but you will still have your days.

Some siblings don't so much resent their siblings as they take care of them. At some point they even start to be the decisions makers for their siblings. They take care of them and become a big help with their autistic sibling. They are eventually the autistic sibling's best friend and sometimes their biggest support.

Either way your neurotypical child feels about having a special needs child the most important thing is to always make the 'normal' child feel just as important as their sibling. Praise them all the time and make sure to educate them as to what autism is and how it affects their sibling. If you have any more questions about this topic the best advice I can give is to research it. With autism the only thing you can really do to get answers to an issue is to turn to articles written by parents and reach out to other parents via support groups. You will not regret it.

Chapter 10

The Dark Side of Caregiver Stress

"I have to admit that I'm suffering from a severe case of battle fatigue," Kelli Stapleton wrote on her online blog one day in September 2013. She used this blog as an outlet and to chronicle the challenges of raising her 14-year-old daughter, Isabelle, who sometimes had violent outbursts like many other autistic children. It is noted in media reports that Kelli had vented on her blog the day of this incident about how wore she was and how much she needed help.

Kelli who was 45, and Isabelle were found unconscious from carbon monoxide poisoning from Kelli lighting charcoal inside the van. Isabelle was hospitalized in critical condition. The incident was determined to be a murder/suicide due to care giver stress. Said her father, Matt Stapleton in an email relayed to the media. (nbcnews.com)

In December 2013 police in an Alabama town identified a woman who was the victim in fatal fire, they couldn't find her son in the home. Police ruled the woman's child Randle's death as a homicide from drowning. The mother, Delicia's, death was ruled suicide from smoke inhalation. This incident was blamed on caregiver stress.

(nbcnews.com)

A former pathologist, Karen McCarron, was sentenced to 36 years in prison for the 2008 suffocation of her 3-year-old daughter, Katherine.

January 2008 Karen was convicted of two counts of first-degree murder, one count of obstructing justice and one count of concealment of a homicidal death. Katie was autistic. In a taped confession, McCarron said that she 'wanted a life without autism.' Her incident was blamed on caregiver stress.

(nbcnews.com)

Wendolyn Markcrow couldn't handle the stress of caring for her 12 year old son, Patrick. His continuous sleeping problems and outbursts drove her over the edge. One day when he wouldn't sleep and the pills she gave him didn't work her solution was to get a plastic bag and put it over his head. Originally she denied doing it but later she confessed. She told police that while she was suffocating him she was shouting at him to be quiet and after she was done she continued to scream it. "I just snapped, I went crazy, I did not know what I was doing." was said during the interrogation.

These are 4 examples of what can happen when a parent is left with no support network, no one to turn too. Most people don't sign up to be a special needs parent. Most of us are just regular people who are going down a different path than we expected. We're flexible, we're tolerant, we're strong, and we're vigilant not in spite of our children, but because of them. Sometimes when it becomes too much a person snaps. The key is finding a way to provide support to the parents through the school system or the police department/emergency services.

The other side of the stress of autism is marital issues. The rate of divorce is rumored to be much higher in parents of autistics. The reasons for divorce normally include the father not helping and money issues. It's very important to have a support system. To research autism online and don't forget we need to research the affects autism on parents as well. Find parents that understand and never be afraid to ask for help, and never forget there is a good side to autism as well. The joy's that come along with this disorder are vast.

Chapter 11

The Joys of Being an Autism Parent

As I mentioned in the last chapter, remembering the joys of raising our children is very important. You have to remind yourself of the good times or you'll never be able to make it through the bad times. I asked several parents to give examples of the joys they have experienced while caring for their autistic child. Getting a real world perspective on it may help you understand that to us even the smallest achievement means the whole world.

Crystal has custody of her autistic grandson. She wants to share that not long ago he did the dishes by hand and he also helped clean his room. Both of those actions are huge. It takes kids years to learn how to do chores or to help us do chores.

Valerie spoke of the first time she heard her 9 year old say mommy. It happened a couple of years ago. They were swimming, Out of nowhere she heard the sweetest little voice say "mommy! Wait!" Needless to say she waited and later cried and laughed all at the same time. She says she gave him the biggest hug. This is one of the most significant moments on the path of raising autism.

Robyn indicated that she was having a 'pity' party for herself. Her son must have heard her crying. He came over, wiped her tears away and said, "Don't be sad mommy you're my best friend". How sweet is that? How monumental. This joy warms your heart to the core.

Judy shared that her son always instinctively knows the right moments to say, sing, or draw unique quotes/pics that match the current situation. He was unaware of. This makes her smile every time.

Quinda spoke of when her grandson was about 12. They took him to the seaside for the weekend. On the way home they were telling each other how much fun they had and she said to him "promise me one thing that you will never be too old to come and stay with us" quick as a flash he came back with, "Grandma I think I will stop coming when you're dead" Like Quinda said, what can you say to that?

Candie shared the day in February that her 10 year old kissed her for the first time. She exclaimed that she will never forget that moment.

Shawntae spoke of when her 8 year old son competed in track. His first season of track. In the events he won five 1st place ribbons and one 2nd place. He was the only special needs kid out there of about 70 kids. He struggled the first few weeks of practice but by the end all the kids knew him and cheered for him during his races. She is so proud of her son because of this.

Leisa said that it was important for her family to know that her child knew they love her. She wasn't showing any recognition of their love. The first time she said I Love you Daddy and kissed him was a life change moment. She felt like she got in. They first sign of affection is often waited for years. Some have to wait years for their joy and some it takes as little as a few months.

Judi spoke of the first time her son showed her affection as well. Her son said 'I love you" for the first time. It reduced her to tears because she never thought she'd hear that phrase. She had longed for it and finally had it. She spoke of watching her son playing with the neighbor's cat as well. He was so innocent and was having so much fun. He would reach down and tell the cat he loved it.

There are so many more reasons and joys to add to the list of positive aspects of autism. Too many to list on one list surely. Days like these, moments like these are rewards for all autism parents.

Chapter 12

Advice from Fellow Autism Parents

As much information as was provided to you in this book so far the best advice you'll ever get is from the parents that have walked this path. The ones that have fought this battle. The parents that have succeed in redefining normal.

Members of an international autism support group were asked to share advice they would give to a new parent of an autistic child. Many of the answers that were given ended up applying to all autism parents. The parents asked are seasoned special needs parents. They are the ones that hold the real world advice that you will need. No doctor or therapist's advice is better or more accurate than the parents that lay down and wake up to the autism in their life. There is no better way to end this book than to leave you with advice you can use. The goal of writing this book was to help, prepare, and guide parents of autistic children along their path. This is what they had to say:

The best advice you could ever be given:

Research

The first person that gave their opinion was a gentleman named Ian. Ian is from Wales. He has an autistic son, not only that Ian himself is a high functioning autistic individual. He is also one of the administrators of the autism group that was asked to participate. Ian's advice to everyone is that in the very beginning a lot of research can be quite dangerous. It could be overpowering and even depressing. He added that you should aim your research at the things the doctors have indicated to be relevant to YOUR child! Don't over work yourself, he indicates, just some research each day. He also advised that you only add more research topics when you have fully absorbed the last bit! He finished up by adding this, "Did I do the above??? NO - of course I didn't! But I wish I had!"

A gentleman named Sam followed Ian up by also recommending parents do research. He also suggested that you remain calm and remember that everybody is different. Heidi also suggested parental research to learn about what they are facing. She also said that it is essential that parents find support from other autism parents. I agree with her 100%.

Awareness and Advocating

Judi came next. Judi lives in Australia. Judi is an author and a great fountain of information when it comes to autism. She suggested that the parents have a laminator. Another great bit of advice I heard from her was that you put the hook side of Velcro to keep pictures up. Judi's last bit of advice was for all autism parents to remember that they are the experts when it comes to their child, no one else.

Ignorance

There were a few members that gave advice a lot of parents do not think of. One of those bits of advice was given from a woman named Marilyn. Marilyn is from California and has raised her sons to adulthood. She addressed a very common problem we all face, the ignorance of family members. The one's that think it is just bad parenting or a behavioral problems with the kids. When her sons were diagnosed she provided her family and friends with info on Autism. Then she arranged to have her immediate and extended family meet in a group with the diagnosing physician. Her family didn't believe the diagnosis.

A member named Donald suggested that new parents be prepared to pick their battles with their child. Remember that some things you have to keep working on. Sometimes though it's just not worth fighting it and you have to let them do it their way. However, be prepared to fight with schools tooth and nail to get your child the support he/she needs. Be prepared for the looks of other people that have no clue and just think your child is a beast. Also, be prepared to want to give up. You have to keep plotting on it because dammit it's your baby and you'll move heaven and earth for him/her. He says to be prepared for absolute frustration from you and your child but also for the signs of ultimate love. Those are what makes everything OK.

Doctors are not Always Right

 Several members advised against instantly believing a professional. You should always get other opinions and go with the one that best fits your situation. Professionals can cause a great amount of damage when allowed to do what they want to treat a child.

The Diagnosis doesn't Change the Child

I am going to quote what a woman named Molly said, the advice she wanted to give. "Your child is being diagnosed by strangers in a strange building for an extremely limited amount of time in a strange room with strange toys. Nothing is familiar, he/she won't be either. They aren't seeing something you have missed all along. You know your kid, they don't. The diagnosis is a word, it's a word that labels a SPECTRUM of children. The diagnosis will bring your kid assistance - disability, early intervention & so on. That is what the "diagnosis" gets you, that's what the word gets you. Don't feel obligated to share your news. You will find support in sharing your new world when you are ready. Support is essential. If you can find people in the same world that you have just entered try to keep them close, they are invaluable. No child on the spectrum is alike. You will learn so much that your brain will explode - just don't let your kid get lost in that fog, he/she is still the same person. Only now you know that he/she is going to allow you to be a part of an entirely new world. Your kid is about to hand you an entirely new perspective on life. One that is completely unique to him/her. That doesn't make your kid special, it makes them extraordinary." Those words are definitely words of wisdom.

I loved what Molly said. She pointed out that the diagnosis doesn't change the child. You still have the same child you always had. Autism just allows you to have a better understanding of the child and better resources to help your child. But your child is still the same child even after the diagnosis. Don't give up hope. Molly added that her son has come further than anyone (but her) thought he could. She never doubted him and knows he will hit his milestones. It just takes him a little longer. Make sure to celebrate all the little things. What seems so little to some people are major steps for us! Molly is so right. We have to cherish all the little things, mostly because they worked so hard to accomplish whatever it is that you are cherishing at the time.

Diet

I spoke to another member named Mary. Mary touched on a subject I hoped would be brought up. The diet of our children. She made it clear that she wished someone would have told her not to stress. She wishes the advice that her sons only eat certain things and as long as they are eating it is fine! She use to stress to the point of tears because her sons always ate the same things. She added that as time has went by they are trying more things. That should give hope to all the new special needs parents that are struggling with this problem. A lot of times this refusal to eat anything but certain foods is a sensory problem. They don't like how the food smells, or how the food feels in their mouths. A lot of parents use pedia-sure to make sure their children are getting the nutrients they need.

Sleep or a Lack There Of

One of the biggest problems of autism parents is sleeping problems. Some children get up several times a night. Some can't fall asleep, some can't stay asleep. A few kids don't have normal REM cycles. Treating this problem is a big issue for parents and doctors. A lot of the time every medication that doctors try don't work. Some medicines like melatonin work. You should always take a moment to lay down and rest during the day. The second bit of advice is to go to an ear, nose, and throat doctor to check and see if your child has sleep apnea.

You can't get any better advice then you got from these amazing parents. They took their time to help you by sharing the things that they have learned on their journey. This goes right back to the importance of a support network. Sometimes the people that 'get you', that help you the most, that understand your tears because they have cried them too you will never meet. That doesn't make them any less valuable.

The reason I wrote this book was to help parents accept their child's diagnosis, handle the schools, the emotions they feel, the stress of this disorder, the horrible results of caregiver fatigue, and to help with a small part of the medical terms and facts. Most if not all new autism parents do not know where to go. They feel alone. 1 in 50 school age kids are on some level of the autistic spectrum. With that statistic imagine how many parents are out there that just wish they could have support.

We parents of autistic individuals have become a strong force of parents. Only the strong survive. Only the empathetic can be part of our family. We have all kinds of different ideas, but when it comes to the bottom line we all have each other's backs. We all want to help each other navigate down the path we were given. The path we love. Having a child with autism most certainly changes the dynamics of your family and most importantly it changes you. Living this life is not easy. Redefining normal is one of the hardest and most rewarding journey's you will ever take. In the end we are all left with no explanation and no answers. We are left at the mercy of the government and foundations that aim towards autism awareness.

It seems researchers are more focused on curing autism then they are with figuring out what caused it and giving closure to the most essential answer we will ever get. The answer we all seek, the reason why this book even needed to be written. Many wonder if we are looking at a new kind of generation. One void of social skills and impulse control. One containing meltdowns and stimming.

These things are just quirks that make up part of your child. Raising autism has its challenges, but, it also has the most emotional appreciation for every hug, every smile, and every instance of eye contact as well. These things will be your smile. Your sense of solace. And anytime you need a little comfort we would be happy to say, "Welcome to the family".

About the Author

Brooke is a 30 year old author from Indiana. She currently

lives in Washington. She's the mother of 2 beautiful little boys and she's been a wife for over a decade, they are her life, her passion. Brooke's the author that never knew she was an author. She's the mother that never thought she'd be a mother and the wife that never thought she'd be a wife.

Not only is her oldest son Autistic. Through support groups and research it's been possible for her to cope, now she wants to repay their generosity by hopefully helping another parent of an autistic child understand what is going on with their child. Brooke has written "Living Through Autism's Eyes: My Journey with My Son", "Simple Steps to IEP Success", "Beautiful Disasters: A Look Inside of Bipolar Disorder", and Melting Down Meltdowns: When a Tantrum isn't a Tantrum.

WORKS CITED

(n.d.). Retrieved from autismfamilycircus.blogspot.com.

(n.d.). Retrieved from wikipedia.com.

(n.d.). Retrieved from Healthline.com.

(n.d.). Retrieved from Webmd.com.

(n.d.). Retrieved from Genetics.thetech.org.

(n.d.). Retrieved from Iancommunity.com.

(n.d.). Retrieved from NIMH.com.

(n.d.). Retrieved from researchautism.net.

(n.d.). Retrieved from autism.about.com.

(n.d.). Retrieved from autism.com.

(n.d.). Retrieved from autismspeaks.org.

(n.d.). Retrieved from Vactruth.com.

(n.d.). Retrieved from blogs.redorbit.com.

(n.d.). Retrieved from myfoxal.com.

(n.d.). Retrieved from nbcnews.com.

(n.d.). Retrieved from ezinearticles.com.

(n.d.). Retrieved from Yourfamilyclinic.com.

POST
HOPE

nationalautism.org

Picture Courtesy of Google Image

special needs moms
A look inside

You may think us "special moms" have it pretty rough.
We have no choice. We just manage life when things get really tough.
We've made it though the days we thought we'd never make it through.
We've even impressed our own selves with all that we can do.

We've gained patience beyond measure, love we never dreamed of giving.
We worry about the future but know this "special" life's worth living.
We have bad days and hurt sometimes, but we hold our heads up high.
We feel joy and pride and thankfulness more often than we cry.

For our kids, we aren't just supermoms. No, we do so much more.
We are cheerleaders, nurses, and therapists who don't walk out the door.
We handle rude remarks and unkind stares with dignity and grace.
Even though the pain they bring cannot be erased.

Therapies and treatment routes are a lot for us to digest.
We don't know what the future holds but give our kids our best.
None of us can be replaced, so we don't get many breaks.
It wears us out, but to help our kids, we'll do whatever it takes.

We are selfless, not by choice, you see. Our kids just have more needs.
We're not out to change the world, but want to plant some seeds.
We want our kids accepted. That really is our aim.
When we look at them we just see kids. We hope you'll do the same.

-April Vernon

Picture Courtesy of Google Images

www.ingramcontent.com/pod-product-compliance
Lightning Source LLC
Chambersburg PA
CBHW070315290526
45791CB00003B/1118